EXPLOSIVE
MAD

Edited by
Albert B. Feldstein

WARNER BOOKS

A Warner Communications Company

When last we saw the beloved Minestrone Family three years (and a couple of hundred bodies, and several Academy Awards, and $100 million in box office grosses) ago, God had made Vino, the original Odd Father, an offer he couldn't refuse and called him to that "Great Pizzeria In The Sky," and Micrin, Vino's youngest son, had taken over. We pick up the action again with Micrin Minestrone as Head of the Family and determined to prove that *he* can play . . .

THE ODD FATHER PART, TOO!

ARTIST: MORT DRUCKER   WRITER: LARRY SIEGEL

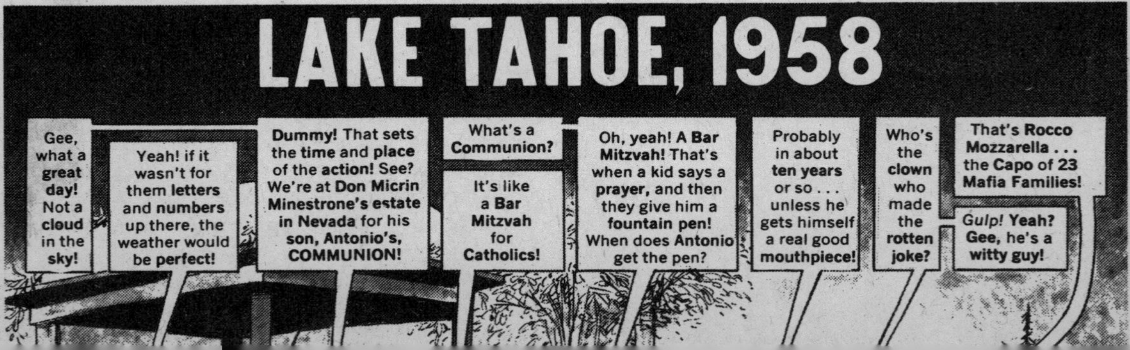
LAKE TAHOE, 1958
Gee, what a great day! Not a cloud in the sky!
Yeah! if it wasn't for them letters and numbers up there, the weather would be perfect!
Dummy! That sets the time and place of the action! See? We're at Don Micrin Minestrone's estate in Nevada for his son, Antonio's, COMMUNION!
What's a Communion?
It's like a Bar Mitzvah for Catholics!
Oh, yeah! A Bar Mitzvah! That's when a kid says a prayer, and then they give him a fountain pen! When does Antonio get the pen?
Probably in about ten years or so . . . unless he gets himself a real good mouthpiece!
Who's the clown who made the rotten joke?
That's Rocco Mozzarella . . . the Capo of 23 Mafia Families!
Gulp! Yeah? Gee, he's a witty guy!

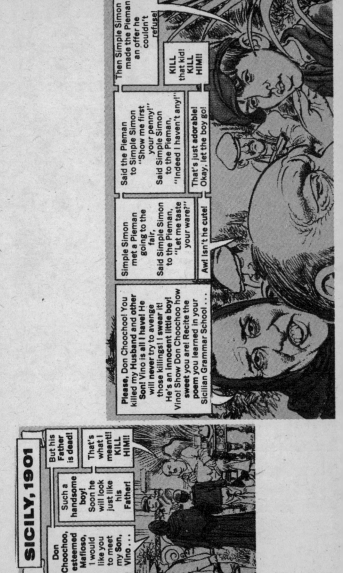

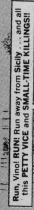
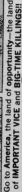

LAKE TAHOE, 1959

It's great being home, Tim! But I missed being here for the Holidays! So give me a run-down! What did you get my Son, Antonio, as a Christmas present from me?

Detroit!

Kids nowadays are spoiled rotten! When I was a kid, the most my Father ever got me was Staten Island!

Well, there goes Freako! And there goes the hotel deal!

Hey, everybody! I think this is turning into a Surprise Party!

Oh, yeah? What's the surprise?

SURPRISE!!

And there goes the country!

WASHINGTON, D.C. 1959

Mr. Minestrone, you have been called before this Senate Committee because we are determined to wipe out the cancer that is threatening to destroy America in the '50's! State your name and line of work . . . and no lying!

I am Micrin Minestrone! I am the Capo of Capos in the Mafia! I control all prostitution, gambling and narcotics in this country. I deal in extortion, blackmail and murder! And I won't stop until the whole world is mine!

No . . . I swear it!

Thank you, and God bless you!

Mr. Minestrone, stop stalling! Are you now, or have you ever been a Communist?

Micrin, things are piling up! You got scores to settle with Herman Roth and Freako . . . and now a Senate Investigating Committee wants you to appear before them in Washington!

A Senate Committee? Uh-oh!! That could mean the end of our whole operation! By the way, who owns Washington?

I think we got a fighting chance!

Your daughter, Maria! You got it for her last Christmas!

NEW YORK CITY, 1925

ONE DAY LAST APRIL

THE
LIGHTER
SIDE OF...

HANDI

CRAFTS

ARTIST & WRITER:
DAVE BERG

...ay I have the **honor** of being the **first one** to **walk** on it?

...u **certainly may** . . .

. . . if you can walk on **WALLS!!**

After my **skiing** accident, I just sat around **doing nothing**! It was driving me **NUTS**!!

Then my **Doctor** suggested that I try making **Wire Sculptures**! So I bought a kit with this **picture** outlined on a **board**! First, I hammered **nails** all around the picture outline . . .

Then I started weaving the wire from nail to nail, in all kinds of **intricate** and **complicated** patterns . . .

Now, you not only have **decorative** objects . . . but it's also **very** therapeutic!

Therapeutic, my foot! It's driving me **NUTS**!

The **Soap Box Derby** is a **fine** idea! It teaches young people **craftsmanship** . . . and **sportsmanship**!

Just take a look at my kid's entry! Note the **graceful design** and the **careful workmanship!** Neat, eh? That's 'cause I helped him **build** it!

That's my kid's entry! I **didn't** help him at all!

And it **sure shows** it! That's pretty sloppy workmanship! You **should** have helped him! A kid his age is **very vulnerable!** His **ego** could be **shattered!**

I really **don't** think so!

HE WON THE RACE!!

Oh, look what Michael **made** today in **Kindergarten**! It's a beautiful replica of a **one-masted sailing schooner**!

No, it's not!!

Of course it isn't! It's a magnificently-crafted model of a **707 jet airliner** . . . !

Nahhh!

What do **young** parents know! Any **Grandma** could recognize that it's a **Frank Lloyd Wright Architectural House**!

Gee! You grown-ups don't know **NUTHIN'**!

David Berg

It's a piece of **wood** . . . with a **nail** in it!

In order to identify themselves as members of certain military, social, sporting, environmental, ethnic and other special groups, many people proudly wear Shoulder Patches. Some people even wear Shoulder Patches and they don't belong to any group. But we're not concerned with those clods. What we are concerned with are the people who belong to certain groups and who do not wear Shoulder Patches because there aren't any. It's for these clods that we've designed this special collection of...

MAD SHOUl

HARASSED WAITRESSES

ARTIST: BOB CLARKE   WRITER: PAUL PETER PORGES

DER PATCHES

THERE AIN'T

NO SUCH THING!

MAFIA MEMBERS

JEWISH MOTHERS

ALL-AMERICAN BIGOTS

SLUM LANDLORDS

LOSING COACHES

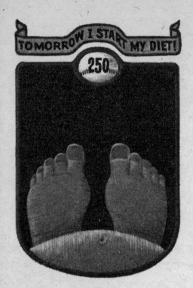

FAT PEOPLE

CHRONIC HYPOCHONDRIACS

NOSEY KID BROTHERS (OR SISTERS)

AGGRESSIVE INSURANCE SALESMEN

DOG-HATING CITY DWELLERS

DONT PACK ME IN !

SUBWAY OR BUS RIDERS

GETTING

INVOLVED

ARTIST & WRITER: SERGIO ARAGONES

The Airline Industry is in serious financial trouble. Because of inflation, operating costs, such as fuel, food, personnel and fancy services, have skyrocketed. However, because of the recession, it is no longer possible to pass these increases on to the passengers. And so, in order to make air travel cheaper and thus attractive to more people, something called "No-Frills Flying" has been introduced. This plan offers lower fares for a more austere type of air travel in which some of the fancy services such as "meals" have been eliminated. If the economic crunch continues and the idea catches on, we may soon be seeing these...

FUTURE "NO-FRILLS" AIR TRAVEL GIMMICKS

ARTIST: AL JAFFEE

WRITTEN BY:
DICK DE BARTOLO &
AL JAFFEE

"FRILL-FREE" STANDING ROOM PASSENGERS

Cost-conscious travelers will be offered "No-Frills Standee Accommodations" which consists of flying erect from point to point securely tucked into their Standing Room Safety Belts.

"FRILL-FREE" OVERHEAD RACK PASSENGERS

Overhead Rack space will be made available to passengers who do not care to stand coast-to-coast, and will happily settle for the cramped "No-Frills Individual Cubicle Accommodations."

"FRILL-FREE" CARGO CONTAINER PASSENGERS

Most economical of all money-saving plans will make use of Cargo Container Holds, where the budget-minded air traveler will be offered "No-Frills Individual Crate Accommodations."

"FRILL-FREE" ROUGH RIDE TREATMENT

Common Air Sickness Trough for "No-Frills" passengers will eliminate need for expensive Individual Air Sickness Bags, and will also eliminate cost of removing used (ecch) bags.

"FRILL-FREE" TOILET ACCOMMODATIONS

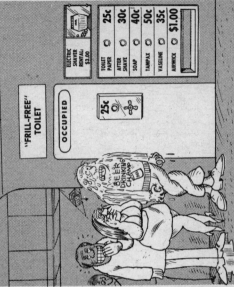

Fancy Johns with free goodies like soap and French perfume will be out for "Frill-Free" passengers. One "Pay Toilet" with "Coin-Operated Necessity-Dispenser" will be available.

"FRILL-FREE" BAGGAGE HANDLING

All "Frill-Free" passengers will be required to store their own luggage aboard the aircraft before flight, and will also be required to retrieve it upon arrival at destination.

"FRILL-FREE" EATING ACCOMMODATIONS

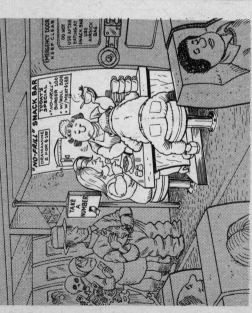

Since costly gourmet meals will be eliminated, a "Frill-Free" Snack Bar" will be installed for use by "Frill Free" passengers. Unfortunately, Snack Bar will only seat two at a time.

"FRILL-FREE" EMERGENCY EQUIPMENT

Airlines now provide costly Life Vests and Emergency Oxygen equipment. "Frill-Free" passengers will be satisfied with simple-to-understand Swimming Instructions and an Air Tube.

HOW AIRLINES CAN INCREASE REVENUES AND PROFITS

IN ADDITION TO

"FUTURE 'NO-FRILLS' AIR TRAVEL GIMMICKS",

HERE ARE SOME OTHER MAD IDEAS ON....

INTERCHANGEABLE PASSENGER ACCOMMODATION EQUIPMENT

300 OR MORE PASSENGERS

100 OR MORE PASSENGERS

30 OR MORE PASSENGERS

ONE PASSENGER

Obviously airlines lose plenty when 6 people fly jets that normally seat 365 and require crews of 18. With this new system, airlines will only use the equipment necessary to accommodate the exact number of passengers that show up.

RENTAL OR LEASING OF VALUABLE BOARDING APRON SPACE

To raise additional revenue valuable runway boarding space can be rented to Concessionaires who will sell everything from local souvenirs to fake photos of "No-Frill" passengers sitting in what looks like the First Class Section on board.

FRANCHISED PASSENGER SERVICES

Airlines can save millions by eliminating all free meals, and then earn additional revenues by selling franchises to Concessionaires who would supply passengers with food.

SALES OF INTERIOR AD SPACES

Eliminating free newspapers and magazines would save money, and then the airlines can earn additional income by selling spaces for ads...which bored passengers will eagerly read.

COIN-OPEATED SEAT DISPENSERS

COIN OPERATION FOR SEAT 6-B	
SAFETY BELT FASTENED	25¢
SAFETY BELT RELEASED	25¢
EMERGENCY PROCEDURES AND A	
DIAGRAM OF EMERGENCY EXITS	50¢
BARF BAG	50¢ (3 for $1)
OVERHEAD READING LIGHT	50¢
AIR CONDITIONING	$1.00
MUSIC	50¢
SNACK TABLE RENTAL	$1.00
PILLOW RENTAL	$2.00
BLANKET RENTAL	$3.00
COMBO/BLANKET/PILLOW	$4.00
ANNOUNCEMENTS FROM CAPTAIN THAT	
MAY CONCERN YOUR LIFE	$2.00

COIN OPERATION FOR SEAT 6-A	
SAFETY BELT FASTENED	25¢
SAFETY BELT RELEASED	25¢
EMERGENCY PROCEDURES AND A	
DIAGRAM OF EMERGENCY EXITS	50¢
BARF BAG	50¢ (3 for $1)
OVERHEAD READING LIGHT	50¢
AIR CONDITIONING	$1.00
MUSIC	50¢
SNACK TABLE RENTAL	$1.00
PILLOW RENTAL	$2.00
BLANKET RENTAL	$3.00
COMBO/BLANKET/PILLOW	$4.00
ANNOUNCEMENTS FROM CAPTAIN THAT	
MAY CONCERN YOUR LIFE	$2.00

Airlines can generate huge revenues by charging for all the services that are now supplied free. A coin operated seat-dispenser will give passenger his choice—for a slight fee.

SELF-SERVICE TICKETING RAMPS

CALIFORNIA
"NO-FRILL" AIR FARE
$9.62
EXACT FARE ONLY
NO PENNIES
CHECKS
CREDIT CARDS
CHANGE

QUARTERS ONLY
COIN BOX

NO-FRILL AIRLINES

Eliminating "Ticket Office" and "Reservation" personnel can effect huge savings. One way airlines can accomplish this is to introduce "Pay-As-You-Enter" ramp-systems for all flights.

REBATE PLANS TO ELIMINATE EXCESS BAGGAGE WEIGHT

Since modern jet planes consume costly fuel in direct proportion to the amount of weight on board, the elimination of excess baggage would mean substantial savings. A system of "No Bag" or "One Bag" rebates could prove very effective.

ONE DAY IN SOUTH DAKOTA

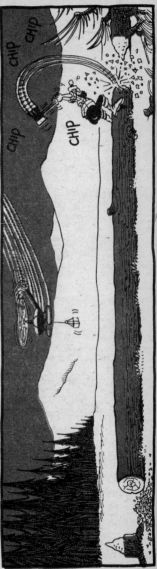

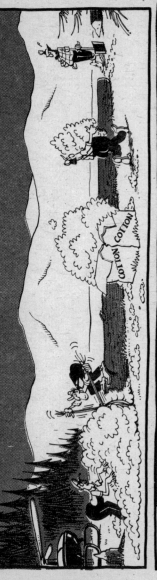

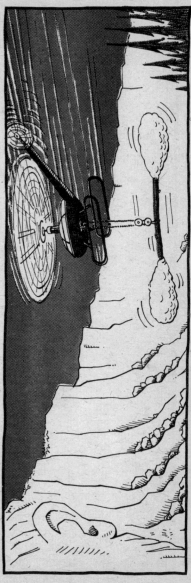

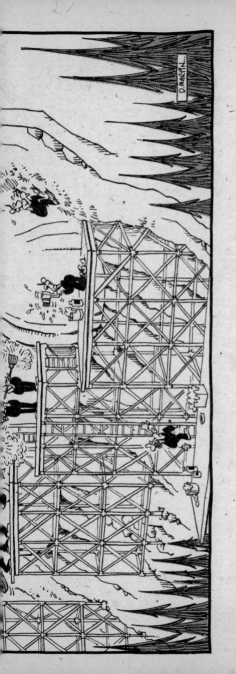

Hi! I'm John Linzey! A vote was taken, and I won the job . . . which may be the **worst** thing for my career since becoming Mayor of New York . . . but I've stupidly accepted this magazine's assignment to interview Mr. Charles Snaffeau who's been named as . . .

MAD'S "TRAFFIC COMMISSIONER" OF THE YEAR

Sorry I'm late! It took me forty minutes to go crosstown!

Driving crosstown in forty minutes isn't bad these days!

Who said anything about DRIVING!?!? I WALKED across town! You can't DRIVE across this town in under two hours!

Then you're AWARE that there's a traffic problem in big cities!

OF COURSE, I'm aware! And I'm not sitting idly by! For example, you see THIS terrible traffic jam? Well, when my men get through, all these double and triple parked cars will be gone!

You'll have them all towed away?

No, I'll have them DRIVEN away! These cars belong to my men! They double and triple parked them so they could look the situation over!

ARTIST: JACK DAVIS   WRITER: DICK DE BARTOLO

It seems like every street in this City is torn up for some reason!

That's not true! There's not one hole dug in Elm Street, and Town Road is free of any construction!

That's good! By the way, Commissioner, where do YOU live?

I live on Elm Street . . . and my office is on Town Road!

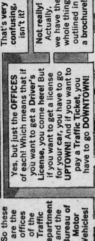

So these are the offices of the Traffic Department and the Bureau of Motor Vehicles!

Yes, but just the OFFICES of each! Which means that if you want to get a Driver's License, you come here! But if you want to get a license for your car, you have to go UPTOWN! And if you want to pay a Traffic Ticket, you have to go DOWNTOWN!

That's very confusing, isn't it?

Not really! Actually, we have the whole thing outlined in a brochure!

Oh? Could I have a copy?

The brochure is only given away at the Traffic Dept. Printing Office . . . CROSSTOWN!!!

TRAFFIC DEPT.
MOTOR VEHICLES

Oh! Is this "Landscaping & Design Dept." responsible for beautifying your City streets?

Well, not exactly . . .

Now here's today's assignments! Too many people can see the "No Left Turn" sign at 2nd and Oak! Plant a bigger bush in front of it! And they're spotting the traffic light on Main at 4th! Re-hang it so it gets lost among the neon signs! And the ivy died that covered the "Stop" sign at—

I see you have some of the new "Picture Regulatory" Road Signs" posted here!

No right turn!
No left turn!
No trucks!
No "U" turn!

Say! What's THIS one? I never saw THIS before! What do these signs forbid . . . ?

Oh, we just put them up around town and let the Arresting Officer decide what should be forbidden at the time!

And this is the Bulletin Board of the "Committee of Traffic Rules and Regulations"! Whenever a new Rule or Regulation is passed by unanimous decision, the public is informed here!

To All Motorists:
Starting Monday,
March 8, 1976,
Franklin Avenue
will be closed
to all traffic!
John Laidlaw
Department of
Re-Surfacing

To All Motorists:
Starting Monday,
March 8, 1976,
Franklin Avenue
will be "One Way"
Southbound!
Richard O. Way
Rights
Director

To All Motorists:
Starting Monday,
March 8, 1976,
Franklin Avenue
will be "One Way"
Northbound!
Noah Sczaman
Asst. Traffic
Manager

Look at the "Parking Meter Dept."! You've got eight men just fixing Parking Meters! But, wait a minute! If they're FIXING them, why are they pounding them with hammers . . . ?!?

They're "fixing" them to pay off better! See, a working Meter only earns 10¢ an hour! But a busted Meter earns at least one $5.00 Illegal Parking Ticket an hour! I mean, the City needs money to operate, and a dime doesn't buy very much these days . . . right!?!?

ONE DAY

WHILE FILMING

A WORLD WAR II

MOVIE

Every year the Postal Service issues a batch of new commemorative stamps, and every year we see the same old kind of subjects. You know—great Presidents, anniversaries of cherished events, renowned scientists, stuff like that. If MAD had it s way, the Postal Service would issue stamps that told it like it really is. Not that it will ever happen! That's why we've titled this article

U.S. COMME

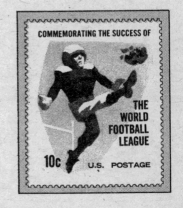

COMMEMORATING THE SUCCESS OF

THE
WORLD
FOOTBALL
LEAGUE

10c   U.S. POSTAGE

MORATIVE STAMPS

STAMPS

That
We'll
Never
Get
To
See

ARTIST: BOB CLARKE
WRITER: FRANK JACOBS

75th ANNIVERSARY OF FIRST
OBSCENE PHONE CALL

MORTON SKEGGS
Cleveland Wierdo

10c

TENTH ANNIVERSARY OF WIFE SWAPPING

1965   1975

AL & TINA, BEN & RHONDA OF YOUNGSTOWN, OHIO

LINDA LOVELACE
Commemorative
$2.00
Deep Blue

KOHOUTEK
COMET OF THE CENTURY
20c

COMMEMORATING THE FIRST POLLUTION OF
LAKE ERIE
11c
2653

HONORING THE TEN MILLIONTH
UNEMPLOYED AMERICAN

NOTICE OF EVICTION

BILLS
NOTICE OF DISMISSAL

10c FAITH HOPE COURAGE DISGUST 10c

Commemorating
THE COLLAPSE OF
THE AMERICAN
DOLLAR
0 c
Gold & Silver

ONE MILLIONTH U.S. MARRIAGE DESTROYED BY WOMEN'S LIBERATION MOVEMENT 1975

5c

U.S. POSTAGE

10th Anniversary
of
School Busing
6 c
Black & White

25th ANiVersary of OBSceNE Graffiti 6¢

SPRAY CAN INVENTOR
MAX WINDRUSH

CELEBRATING **50** YEARS OF **PLANNED OBSOLESCENCE**

2c

1975

TEN YEARS OF RUNAWAY INFLATION

1965

15c

TENTH ANNIVERSARY OF THE

1 9 6 5

1 9 7 5

8c

EAST COAST POWER BLACKOUT

50th Anniversary
**AMERICAN
COMMUNIST PARTY**
3 c
Red

SPIRO T. AGNEW MEMORIAL

Becoming a
household word

1c

SPIRO T. AGNEW MEMORIAL

Denouncing
the press

2c

SPIRO T. AGNEW MEMORIAL

Blaming the
intellectuals

3c

SPIRO T. AGNEW MEMORIAL

Getting
the axe

4c

Saluting America's
Used Car Dealers
7c
Lemon

TOTAL VICTORY

NO CENTS

IN VIET NAM

Howard Johnson
Commemorative
29 c
Chocolate, Vanilla
Strawberry, Cherry,
Peach, Pistachio,
Butter Pecan,
Coffee, etc.

TENTH ANNIVERSARY
OF 500TH DRAFT DODGER
REACHING CANADA
1965   1975

MONTREAL

12c

125th ANNIVERSARY OF

1850   MUGGING OF
FIRST TOURIST
IN NEW YORK CITY   1975

WELDON SCURVY
Vacationing Denver Druggist

18c

HONORING AMERICA'S GROUPIES

LED ZEPPELIN FANATIC
AVA GRUNDLEMAN

5c

SALUTING 20 YEARS OF MAD MAGAZINE

ecchh

1/4c
CHEAP!

A MAD

AT

LOOK BACK-PACKING

ARTIST & WRITER:
SERGIO ARAGONES

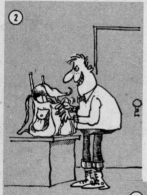

The most frequent criticism of television comes from those who find TV's emphasis on sex and violence to be "an unrealistic depiction of American life." Apparently these critics get so wrapped up watching all that sex and violence that they never even notice the *really dumb* things on TV. Whoo-boy . . . talk about *unrealistic!* MAD invites all the anti-sex and anti-violence people to tell us if they can . . .

WHERE ELSE

ARTIST: JACK DAVIS   WRITER: TOM KOCH

BUT ON

... do pet dogs and their charming masters share the amazing trait of never having to go to the bathroom?

WHERE ELSE BUT ON TV . . .

. . . does a Postman always bring vitally important letters,
but never any unsolicited catalogues or bills or junk mail?

WHERE ELSE BUT ON TV . . .

. . . is it unnecessary for an apartment building to have a directory or an inter-com because there are always twenty gorgeous girls lolling around the pool . . . ready to supply the information (or anything else) a person might desire?

WHERE ELSE BUT ON TV . . .

. . . is there never the nuisance of taking off coats and galoshes because it's never cold or raining? (In fact, there's rarely weather of *any* kind on TV shows, except on Christmas Eve, when it suddenly starts snowing everywhere.)

WHERE ELSE BUT ON TV...

... do people who are eager for details of some specific news event invariably turn on their TV set at the exact moment the report they want to hear is being broadcast?

WHERE ELSE BUT ON TV...

LANDLADIE

... does a Landlady invariably have an I.Q. of 65, except when it comes to remembering the height, weight and hair color of every stranger that visited one of her tenants?

WHERE ELSE BUT ON TV...

. . . can someone, breaking into a strange office in total darkness, never fail to locate that one important piece of evidence that the police couldn't find when they went over the place with a fine tooth comb in broad daylight?

WHERE ELSE BUT ON TV...

. . . can people dial so many calls in frantic haste without ever reaching a wrong number, a busy signal or a recording?

WHERE ELSE BUT ON TV...

... does every hospital maintain a complete spare staff of doctors and nurses that do nothing else but sit around and wait for the next emergency case to be brought in?

WHERE ELSE BUT ON TV...

... is the most profound wisdom dispensed by old duffers who never went to school, never held a job and never even scraped together enough money to buy some new overalls?

WHERE ELSE BUT ON TV...

. . . is a home-made time bomb expected to explode right on the split second, even though it's always attached to the type of cheap alarm clock that is notoriously inaccurate?

WHERE ELSE BUT ON TV...

. . . are planes and boats always completely serviced and ready for instant departure, just waiting for crooks to show up and steal them so they can make their getaways?

WHERE ELSE BUT ON TV...

... does anyone needing to make an emergency call always find himself next to a pay phone that's in working order?

WHERE ELSE BUT ON TV...

... are all hospital patients placed in private rooms with doctors and nurses clamoring to provide service?

WHERE ELSE BUT ON TV...

... is it impossible to find someone who just pumps gas—without being the town character, and/or the hatchet man for the local Sheriff, and/or the front for a drug ring?

WHERE ELSE BUT ON TV...?

... do newspapers ignore things like inflation, wars and unemployment in order to devote their page one headlines to some second-rate crime that almost nobody cares about?

WHERE ELSE BUT ON TV...

... can a person take one quick glance into a rear-view mirror and immediately differentiate between a car that's tailing him and one that just happens to be going his way?

WHERE ELSE BUT ON TV...

... are restaurants staffed with attentive waiters, all eager to run suspicious errands or fink on their closest friends or even (Hah-hah!) take a patron's dinner order?

WHERE ELSE BUT ON TV...

. . . can two cars engage in a 75-mile-an-hour chase through heavy traffic without ever hitting an innocent bystander?

WHERE ELSE BUT ON TV...

. . . can people continue to shoot at each other out of car windows while engaged in a 75-mile-an-hour chase through heavy traffic without ever hitting an innocent bystander?

THE LIGHTER SIDE OF...

THE SUMMER SCENE

ARTIST & WRITER: DAVE BERG

I love the **smells** of Summer! The smell of an **ocean breeze,** tinged with a **fine salt spray!**

The smell of a **flower garden,** perfumed with **vivid blossoms!** The smell of **city sidewalks,** damp from a **brief Summer rain!**

The smell of a **forest glade,** spiced with **pine needles!** The smell of **fresh-cut grass,** sparkling with **morning dew!**

. . . and the smell of a **Locker Room,** pungent with moist sweat socks!!

No wonder your luggage was so heavy! You've got all those BOOKS in there!

These are the books I bought myself over the Winter, but never got to!

Comes Summer vacation time, it's my chance to catch up . . .

I love to relax in the sun and enjoy a good book! When you're relaxed, you can get the MOST out of a book!

ZNNNz

That's what I **hate** about **Summer** sports! They're mostly **so COMPETITIVE!**

Yeah!

Lots of guys have to show off their **Macho!** They have to get their kicks out of **beating** other guys! Well . . . **NOT ME!!**

Me neither!

I just have **NO NEED to compete!**

Same here!

Oh, **yeah?!** I'll bet I'm **less competitive** than **you!**

Pollution Alert

ARTIST & WRITER: SERGIO ARAGONES

There are people who say that the American Class System is dying out ... that America is becoming a "Classless Society." To those people, we say, "Forget it!" The Class System lives, and to help you distinguish who falls into what category, here's

A MAD GUIDE TO THE MODERN AMERICAN CLASS SYSTEM

ARTIST: PAUL COKER, JR.   WRITER: FRANK JACOBS   IDEA BY: MARYLIN D'AMICO

WHEN YOU'RE DOWN AND OUT

You wait in line
at the clinic.

WHEN YOU'RE JUST GETTING BY

You wait in line to see
your family doctor.

WHEN YOU'RE MAKING IT

You're put first in line to
see your family doctor.

WHEN YOU'RE ON TOP OF THE HEAP

Your family doctor waits
in line to see you.

WHEN YOU'RE
DOWN AND OUT

You're for Busing because
you figure that any change
in schools has got to help.

WHEN YOU'RE
JUST GETTING BY

You're against Busing
because the Down-And-
Outers are for it.

WHEN YOU'RE
MAKING IT

You take whatever
view of Busing
is fashionable.

WHEN YOU'RE
ON TOP OF THE HEAP

You're not for or against
Busing, since your kids go
to private schools anyway.

WHEN YOU'RE
DOWN AND OUT

You collect matchbook covers from far-away places like The Trenton Holiday Inn and Al's Bar In Sandusky.

WHEN YOU'RE
JUST GETTING BY

You collect stamps from exotic countries like Outer Mongolia and Tierra del Fuego.

WHEN YOU'RE
MAKING IT

You collect tropical fish from South-Sea paradises like Tahiti and American Samoa.

WHEN YOU'RE
ON TOP OF THE HEAP

You collect common stock certificates from dull old companies like General Motors and U.S. Steel.

WHEN YOU'RE
DOWN AND OUT

You peep at X-rated
movies in penny arcades.

WHEN YOU'RE
JUST GETTING BY

You watch X-rated
movies in theaters.

WHEN YOU'RE
MAKING IT

You rent X-rated movies
and show them at home.

WHEN YOU'RE
ON TOP OF THE HEAP

You date
the star.

WHEN YOU'RE
DOWN AND OUT

You vote for the
politician who promises
to increase Welfare.

WHEN YOU'RE
JUST GETTING BY

You vote for the
politician who promises to
preserve neighborhoods.

WHEN YOU'RE
MAKING IT

You vote for the
politician who promises
to lower taxes.

WHEN YOU'RE
ON TOP OF THE HEAP

You vote for
the politician
you own.

WHEN YOU'RE DOWN AND OUT

You can't afford to worry about being in fashion . . . and besides, nobody cares how you look anyway.

WHEN YOU'RE JUST GETTING BY

You think you're in fashion, but you're not—because the discount store you buy from is 3 years behind the times.

WHEN YOU'RE MAKING IT

You wear whatever's "In" and "Now"—regardless of cost so that everyone else Making It will know **you're** Making It.

WHEN YOU'RE ON TOP OF THE HEAP

Whatever you wear is "In"— **or else!**

WHEN YOU'RE
DOWN AND OUT

You own a '66 Volkswagen
and you have your eye
on a '71 Chevrolet.

WHEN YOU'RE
JUST GETTING BY

You own a '71 Chevrolet
and you have your eye
on a '76 Gremlin.

WHEN YOU'RE
MAKING IT

You own a '76 Oldmobile
and you have your eye
on a '77 Mercedes.

WHEN YOU'RE
ON TOP OF THE HEAP

You own a '21 Pierce-Arrow
and you have your eye
on a '06 Reo.

WHEN YOU'RE DOWN AND OUT

You let your daughter hear the Rolling Stones on the radio for her 16th Birthday . . . after you're through listening to the ball game.

WHEN YOU'RE JUST GETTING BY

You give your daughter a Rolling Stones record album for her 16th Birthday.

WHEN YOU'RE MAKING IT

You buy your daughter front-row seats for a Rolling Stones live concert for her 16th Birthday.

WHEN YOU'RE ON TOP OF THE HEAP

You hire the Rolling Stones to entertain at your daughter's Sweet Sixteen Birthday Party.

WHEN YOU'RE
DOWN AND OUT

You don't think
about the past or
the future, being
too worried about
the present.

WHEN YOU'RE
JUST GETTING BY

You wonder what you could
have done in the past to
improve the present that's
been giving you so many
worries about the future.

WHEN YOU'RE
MAKING IT

You hope the future
will be as much of an
improvement on the
present as the present
has been on the past.

WHEN YOU'RE
ON TOP OF THE HEAP

You couldn't
care less
about
the whole
thing.

WHEN YOU'RE DOWN AND OUT

You scream at your wife
for overspending.

WHEN YOU'RE JUST GETTING BY

You scream at your wife
for overspending.

WHEN YOU'RE MAKING IT

You scream at your wife
for overspending.

WHEN YOU'RE ON TOP OF THE HEAP

You scream at your wife
for overspending.

EARLY
ONE
MORNING
DOWNTOWN

As if pictures like "Earthquake" and "Jaws" and "Towering Inferno" aren't scary enough, Hollywood has now devised a new type of film that shows how terrible life will be like in the future . . . if you're lucky enough not to be crushed to death, bitten to death or burned to death! Here's MAD's version of tomorrow's spectator sport:

ROLLERBRAWL

ARTIST:
ANGELO TORRES

WRITER:
STAN HART

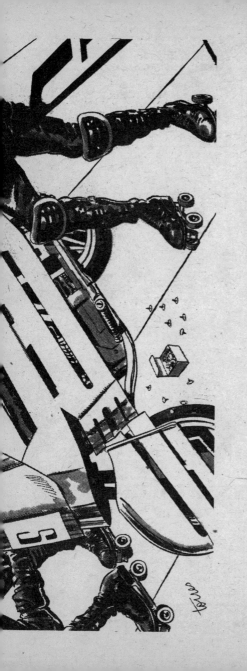

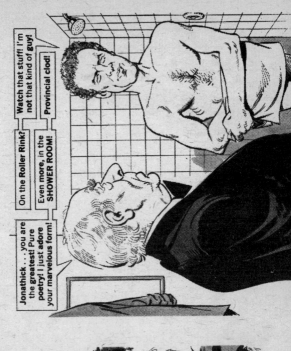

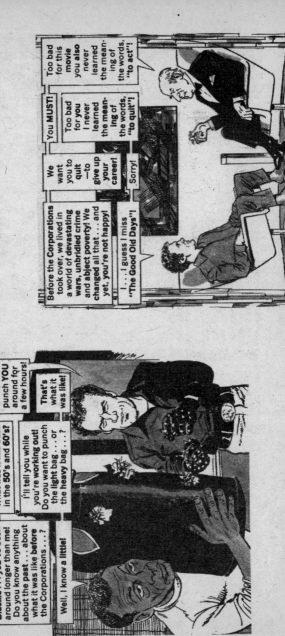

That heavy speeding ball is going to tear your head off!

No . . . ! No . . . !

Come on! It's all part of the game! Nothing personal!

Oh, good! For a minute, I thought you were mad at me!

Pardon my glove!!

Stop slouching!!

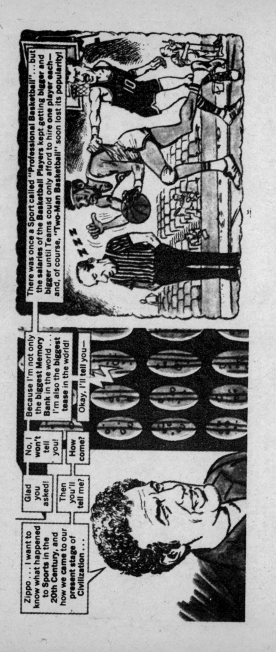

Once upon a time, there were two men . . . Frank Gifford and Howard Cosell . . . who killed a Sport called "Professional Football" by **confusing the fans!** After Gifford would tell them how **wonderful** everything was, Cosell would tell them how **stupid** they were for enjoying it!

There was also a Sport called "Professional Baseball" . . . in which financially ailing Teams would occasionally switch their franchises from one city to another to get more paying customers! Then, they started switching more and more often —every year—then every week—until the fans couldn't tell from one day to the next if their city had any Team at all!

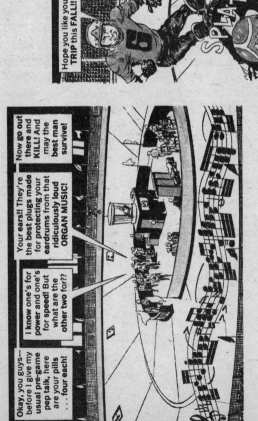

ONCE UPON A TIME
IN THE

BLACK HILLS
OF S. DAKOTA

floof